I Never Got Laid
In A Restaurant

Global High Praise for Bent Tines
And His Culinary Approach

"I find irresistible a man who knows his way around the kitchen. He displays competence, sensitivity, sensuality and command—things that transfer well to the bedroom, as Bentley has amply demonstrated."

– Sarah E.-M., London

"He came, he sautéed, he conquered."

– Sophia G., Rome

"My ideal man knows the culinary, and he is like a god: a creator with the knowledge and beauty of Apollo, the drunken madness of Dionysus, the sensuality of Eros. Follow Bent's recipe for pleasure and you will see."

– Christina Z., Athens

"Bent skewered, seared and flambéed—for what more could a Frenchwoman ask?"

– Monique Q de R, Paris

"Bent Tines saw to it that I was well fed and well forked."

– Darlene J., Dallas

I Never Got Laid In A Restaurant

Seven Seductive Dinners for the Culinary Clueless

BY
BENT TINES

APPETITES PRESS

Published in the United States by Appetites Press.

Key West, Florida

I Never Got Laid In A Restaurant:

Seven Seductive Dinners for the Culinary Clueless

ISBN 978-0-9835705-8-5

All photos are original and depict actual results.

www.benttines.com

"Sharing food with another human being is an intimate
act that should not be indulged in lightly."
—*M.F.K. Fisher*

"Great food is like great sex.
The more you have the more you want."
—*Gael Greene*

Contents

An Introduction to Pleasure

Even if one has wads of cash, why waste it on taking women to pricey restaurants where nothing sexually substantive is likely to happen? (Though I did once have something interesting occur beneath a white tablecloth at a toney Italian trattoria. But then she and I were already old friends.) Better to invite her to your place, where most anything can happen. And where you can control the mood and the ambiance, demonstrate your cosmopolitan skills in the highly sensual activities of preparing food and pouring wine, and then spring the trap. A wonderful evening for all, but then I've always been a romantic and a sensualist.

Cooking, like sex, calls on all your senses, with good food and good sex sharing some of the same necessary ingredients—a pleasing presentation, stimulating aromas, appealing textures, great taste, and swallowing.

Asking a lady to dinner at a restaurant in order to get to know her and perhaps (you hope) bed her, is a lame and unimaginative default ploy for many men. But most guys—and I speak here of my book's primary target audience, the beer-swilling sports addict, which includes most all American males—are clueless about women, seduction and seductive food. Like my nephew, a Navy pilot. I once visited him when he was stationed in Key West. On my departure day he told me he had convinced some local blonde to drop by his apartment for dinner that night.

"Great!" I said. "Keeping up the family tradition. What are you serving?"

"Thought I'd throw some brats on the grill, knock back a few brewskis."

I registered disbelief: "Are you, Lieutenant Tines, fucking kidding me? Then what—watch the Packers on TV? The object here is to score, my lad, to flatter and please the lady with your attentions so as to improve the gene pool, or at least go through the motions."

He hung his head. I went on in a more comforting tone:

"Despite the nicely phallic implications of the bratwurst, this sounds like a losing game plan. We need to devise a seductive dinner."

We made a trip to the PX, where we bought some Frenched lamb chops, crusty bread, mixed greens, a nice Bordeaux, a few other ingredients, candles, and the necessary kitchen implements he lacked— including a mortar and pestle. In the mortar we ground some fresh basil and garlic with olive oil to make a heavenly pistou for the chops; I instructed him on the proper preparation of the lamb—so it would be seared on the outside, bloody good on the inside—and gave him some rudimentary instruction about creating a romantic atmosphere, food presentation, and, lastly, tips on how to move from the dining room to loveseat for the ultimate dessert course.

I am happy to report that his date judged Lieutenant Tines suave, sophisticated and thus sexy, and the evening was an arousing success.

If, like my benighted nephew, you are among the culinary clueless, this book is for you. By following my precepts here, you too can parlay prowess in the kitchen into triumph in the boudoir.

Though at the time my nephew was clueless re cooking, at least he had had the good sense—and this could be genetic—to have her over to his place. I'm generally pretty upfront about the invitation, even with someone I just met:

"I'd like to treat you to dinner Saturday. I know somewhere with terrific food, great wine and very, very attentive service."

"Where's that?"

"My place."

Such an invitation, tantamount to a sexual proposition, cuts through a lot of the propriety, b.s. and coy cat-and-mouse game that some females play. If she agrees, she's as good as had—if you know what you're doing in the kitchen. If she declines, nothing's lost. You weeded out someone lacking a sense of adventure and avoided spending a hundred bucks or two on a disappointing restaurant dinner—perhaps without a happy ending, as they say in Chinatown.

Further, in addition to the limited opportunities to get laid in a restaurant, eating out, that is, dining out, boasts other potential drawbacks:

- Having to wait for a table, possibly among a group of loudmouths, drunks, families and/or influenza carriers.

- Risking poor service. A surly, incompetent, overworked, inattentive, or inebriated waiter or waitress can suck all the romance from an expensive dinner. And often they are at the mercy of incompetence, understaffing or hung-over help in the kitchen.

- Getting lousy food. Even good restaurants can serve up second-rate meals, generally by overcooking and over-seasoning the food. And a lot of restaurant fare these days—even at some expensive restaurants—is pre-prepared frozen stuff of dubious provenance.

- Eating tainted food. I never get food poisoning when dining at home, as I don't use seafood that's been sitting around for days, I don't touch myself then touch the food, and I don't sneeze on the salad—all risks when dining out. Though I would not order steak tartare in a restaurant these days, I continue to make and eat it at home with good result (see: Raw Meat for a Savage Carnivore).

- Getting ripped off. Good restaurants generally charge out the wazoo for their fare, four to five times what it costs me to make the same thing at home—and usually I do it much better than they do. Further, the eateries usually treble or quadruple wine prices as well, so you end up drinking lesser wines or paying through the nose. Conversely, cooking at your place you've got low overhead, cheap labor and wine without the markup.

- Having to drink and drive. Obviously not an issue when you're at home. Further, the rigid enforcement of drunk driving laws these days and the risk of getting a costly DUI give your date another reason to spend the night—which is likely what she will want to do anyway after you put her in a sensuous mood with a romantic dinner.

However, to create that romantic mood takes some planning, preparation and knowledge—which I provide in the following pages: a simple guide to compose seven surefire seductive dinners.

I've always maintained that if you know how to read, you can make good meals. In *I Never Got Laid in a Restaurant* I've compressed years of experience in the arts of the kitchen and the couch—and years reading, studying and enjoying food and wine—into a few simple keys and recipes that lead to great eating and great pleasure.

If you like eating well, living well, and fornicating, read on.

Straight from Bent:

A Pansexual Invitation

While this book is written from a decidedly heterosexual man's point of view and aimed at the culinarily benighted male Homo sapiens, women (as well as male and female homosexuals—am I leaving anyone out?) can also enjoy and benefit from its world-wise lessons for the kitchen, dining room and bedroom. In these delightful days of sexual equality and license, it is certainly appropriate for a woman to seduce a man as well as vice versa. (I'd also invite the married man or woman to use my recipes and seduction tactics to add some unexpected spice to a bland marital stew.)

Further, the book offers women a revealing glimpse inside the male sexual psyche, as simple and straightforward as it may be.

Good food, good wine and good sex form a triumvirate of deep pleasure that—happily and appropriately—is best conducted in private. I believe that most of us (waiters and chefs perhaps excluded) can honestly attest, "I never got laid in a restaurant!" The following pages will help you successfully orchestrate that holy trinity of good food, wine and sex.

¡Buen provecho!

I Never Got Laid
In A Restaurant

Chapter 1

"Give a man the right tool and he can do any job."

A lot a guys hate the kitchen. But they have been mis-educated and are missing the boat: The kitchen is a sexy venue where pleasure takes shape.

A lot a guys hate the kitchen. But they have been mis-educated and are missing the boat: The kitchen is a sexy venue where pleasure takes shape.

Some men childishly associate the kitchen with their mothers: cooking is woman's work. Its sexism aside, that notion does not stand up to evidence. Many of the world's great chefs have been men, and many of them profited handsomely by it—both monetarily and sexually. It is time, gentlemen, to detach the apron strings and break from childish notions. When you think kitchen and cooking, don't think "Mom," think "Pussy!"

Cooking, like fooking, can be fun if you do it right. But for both you need to have the proper equipment. (As Father always said, "Give a man the right tool and he can do any job.")

Here are some of the must-have gadgets and accouterment for your kitchen and your dining area. And you can find it all online at Amazon and other retailers, so there's no need to leave the couch to do your seduction outfitting. But if you're on a tight budget, try stocking your kitchen from SallyMae's Boutique (the Salvation Army Store), yard sales and such. Good venues, by the way, to find seasoned cast-iron cookware.

Further, if you think you can get along without any of these items by improvising and being clever, so much the better. Your date will be impressed by your resourcefulness.

For example, I always crack ice for cocktails by hand—the way old-time bartenders did—holding a cube in the palm of my left hand and whacking it with the back of a serving spoon. Inevitably she'll ask:

"Doesn't that hurt?"

"Of course," you say with a blasé shrug.

You see, it is possible to be macho in the kitchen, especially when you start throwing knives around and starting purposeful fires.

For the kitchen:

Corkscrew. Get a simple waiter's knife and learn how to use it so it looks like you know what you're doing. I use a Screwpull®, but there are many good ones. The Wine Enthusiast sells bargain-priced double-hinged waiter's corkscrews on Amazon.com. These implements also open beer and Pellegrino bottles.

- *Garlic press.* Fear not garlic. As long as you both are saturated with it, its highly sensual aroma won't be a turnoff.

- *Sharp knives.* You don't need a costly O.J. Simpson special or a whole set of Wüsthof blades. Just a large carving knife, a serrated blade for slicing and a small paring knife ought to do it. But don't go cheap. Get some heavy metal that will last longer than a season.

- *Cutting board.* Plastic is okay. I prefer wood for its better aesthetics. (Also better for the knife-throwing demonstrations.)

- *Vegetable peeler.* Best to buy this item new, as used ones are likely dulled.

- *Tongs.* Long and strong works best, as with other implements.

- *Whisk.* A small one is sufficient.

- *Flipper.* This is a metal bladed instrument used to flip a steak or an egg. Not to be confused with a spatula, which has a pliable head and is good for scraping bowls and mixing—and which you don't really need, though they are also nice for spanking.

- *A slotted spoon.* For stirring pasta and straining small quantities.

- *Salad spinner.* Not needed if you buy the packaged triple-washed lettuce and spinach.

- *Can opener.* Go manual. I've always used a Swing-A-Way portable—the same model U.S. astronauts took to the moon.

- *A large, two-handled pot, for boiling pasta.* Some even come with strainer lids.

- *A colander.* For draining pasta, veggies, etc.

- *Grater.* For cheese, lemon zest, nutmeg and more. A small one on a handle will do.

- *A cast-iron skillet or two.* Not expensive. If you have the cash you can get a lighter, black-steel skillet. But by all means avoid anything with a nonstick coating, such as Teflon.

- *Grill or grill pan.* The best, inexpensive grill in my experience is the Weber Q—propane-powered with a heavy steel grill. Likewise, the grill pan should be heavy cast iron or steel.

- *A Dutch oven.* Again, cast iron or other heavy metal is good.

- *Smaller pots.* A couple saucepans with lids will suffice. Make sure they have a heavy base that distributes heat evenly. Cheap tin ware will lead the inexperienced cook—and even some kitchen veterans—to burn most everything.

- *Vegetable steamer.* A metal colander can double as a steamer if you're really frugal. I've always used the cheap, folding variety of vegetable steamer.

- *Measuring cup.* Not all that necessary, since you likely have an empty beer bottle around and can estimate stuff—cooking is not an exact science, but an art. You know that a beer is 12 oz. and a cup is 8 oz. and there are 16 tablespoons in a cup. Take it from there.

- *Measuring spoons.* Again, somewhat of an extravagance. I learned to cook from my governess, who never measured anything except when baking or sizing me up. "How much salt do you put in, Monique?"... "Just enough, my salty little devil."

- *Mixing bowls.* Get a large one and a couple smaller ones.

- *Cookie sheet.* Don't worry, brother, you don't have to bake cookies to get laid. (Actually I'd advise against it, unless you're trying to get laid by another guy.) This is for pizza and such.

- *Pepper and salt mills.* Always good to have a little grinding going on in the kitchen. The pepper mill is a must, as freshly ground peppercorns carry much more punch and aroma than the pre-cracked pepper. The salt mill is optional.

- *An electric blender or food processor.* No need to spend 300 bucks on an industrial-strength food processor. A $40 Oster blender will do.

- *Kitchen towels.* Cotton.

- *A barstool,* where she can sit while she observes the chef in action, crossing her legs, hiking her skirt and licking her lips. (I've also found that it's often a short trip from the kitchen stool to the kitchen counter, where she can really kick up her heels.)

Kitchen stuff you DON'T need:

- *Rolling pin.* A wine bottle works just fine and is more masculine and phallic.

- *Thermometer.* We're doing informed intuitive cooking here, an artistic endeavor. We don't need to quantify everything exactly. However, for the kitchen novice it could come in handy for dishes like the Rack of Lamb Provençal.

- *Oven mitts and potholders.* This is what the towels you take from the gym are for—that and polishing your car.

- *Plastic storage containers.* Most every single woman has dozens of these stuffed in her pantry. I fear there exists somewhere a "Plastic Container of the Month Club" that they all subscribe to, or that they are attending Tupperware parties. On top of that they'll have plastic zipper bags in five different sizes. Redundant and unnecessary, all of it. Aluminum foil and a roll of cling wrap are all you need for storage, along with your small mixing bowls and plates.

For the presentation and the dining area:

- *Candles.* Women, romantics at heart mostly, adore a candlelit dining area, even if it's in your tiny kitchen. Candlelight suggests simpler, more primitive times. After all, you're after some primitive pleasure, right? And don't worry about fancy candleholders. An empty wine bottle works fine and adds an air of improvisation and casualness—the last thing you want to come off as is stiff (in the priggish sense), formal and unapproachable. Work to project earthiness.

- *Silverware.* Knives, forks, teaspoons, tablespoons. No need for serving spoons and such.

- *Dishes.*
  - Dinner plates.
  - Salad plates or bowls.
  - Side dish plates.
  - Serving platter.

- *Drinking vessels.*
  - Wine glasses. You'll need two small ones for white wine, two larger goblets for red wine, and two narrow Champagne flutes.
  - Coffee cups.
  - Espresso cups.
  - Water glasses.

- *Cloth napkins and tablecloth.* These work to build the sense of occasion. Further, the napkins can also double as blindfolds, and the tablecloth will prevent splinters if things turn spontaneous.

Chapter 2

A Vegan Repast for a Green Piece

I have no argument with vegans except for the PETA people with the "Meat is murder!" bumper stickers. (The omnivore's riposte: "Vegetables is suicide!")

In fact, I encourage vegetarianism, as it lowers meat prices for the carnivorous amongst us. But I like to cook and eat vegetarian as well—not just every day.

Similarly, like a good scout you should Be Prepared when a tasty vegan crosses your path. And if you are hanging out in campus venues, fern bars or espresso cafes these days, you are likely to encounter one. So you need to have in your repertoire at least a couple seductive meatless dinners (which may lead you to discover that she does have a taste for meat after all, if only on the hoof).

One of my favorite meals—vegan or otherwise—is pasta with pesto sauce: a blend of fresh basil, pine nuts, Parmesan cheese, garlic, and olive oil. Done right, it is fragrant, sensuous and sexy, redolent of earthy aromas and tasting heavenly. Further, it's not that hard to pull off if you know what you are doing.

I prefer using spinach pasta, as they do in Liguria, where the dish originated. Both spinach linguini and spaghetti are readily available in most urban areas. But pesto is also delicious with regular pasta, including rigatoni, farfalle and fettuccine.

Some may argue that this garlic-heavy dish will impede the face-licking foreplay of a romantic evening and thus possibly derail the sexual denouement. But I have found otherwise. When you are both garlicked up, you never notice it. And, as we all know, highly seasoned foods stir that vile lust we harbor and seek.

Spinach Linguine with Pesto

*Tip: Shopping lists of ingredients for each dinner can be found at the end of this book. Snap a picture or tear it out and take it along, making the shopping process oh-so-simple.

Ingredients:

2 cups fresh *basil leaves*.

2 *garlic cloves* processed through a garlic press or chopped fine.

2 tablespoons *pine nuts*. (Note: Try to avoid pine nuts from China. They may come from a different species of pine that can produce a bitter taste that can linger for days. Walnuts may be substituted.)

3/4 cup *extra virgin olive oil*.

Salt and freshly *ground pepper*.

1/2 cup freshly grated *Parmesan cheese*. (Preferably from Italy, the Parmigiano-Reggiano. Domestic Parmesan can be successfully substituted. Italian Pecorino Romano works well, but it is very salty, so you may omit the salt above.)

1 lb. *spinich linguine*. (I usually use the Italian DeCecco brand, as it cooks firmer. And, as noted above, you can successfully use other pastas—most any will be delicious if done right.)

Steps:

- Put the basil leaves, pine nuts, and pressed garlic in a food processor or blender. (Reserve a few basil leaves for garnish.)

- Pulse to chop coarsely.

- Add half the olive oil, half the grated cheese, salt and pepper.

- Blend until pureed. It should have the consistency of a very thick soup. Add more olive oil as necessary.

- Bring 3 gallons of water in a two-handled pot to boiling on high heat.

- Add salt—lots of it, perhaps two fistfuls, say 1/4 cup.

- Slip in the pasta and stir. Now keep an eye on it, stirring occasionally and, after a few minutes, fetching a piece out of the water to test for doneness. You'll want to take it out before it is fully cooked, while still just a bit hard in the center, as it will continue to cook out of the water.

- When the pasta is cooked to perfection, pour the contents in a colander in the sink. Shake to remove excess water.

- In a large mixing bowl stir together half the pesto sauce with the pasta.

- Arrange on individual dinner plates, and don't overdo the portion—it will look unprofessional. A quarter pound is plenty. Spoon a tablespoon or two of the pesto sauce in the center of the serving. Garnish with fresh basil leaves.

Serve with remaining pesto sauce and cheese in bowls on the side.

Fresh tomatoes are a nice accompaniment to the dish—cherry tomatoes artfully arranged on the side of the plate or sliced tomatoes on a side dish.

Although some other wine experts suggest a substantial white wine such as a Burgundy, I generally prefer a light red wine with pesto—perhaps a Valpolicella or Beaujolais. And bottled mineral water—the bubbly stuff, Pellegrino or Perrier, perhaps—which I serve with every dinner.

Also, after dinner you'll be craving something sweet. Some gelato or other ice cream would hit the spot, along with a snifter of Cognac to get everyone nice and relaxed and pliable.

Straight from Bent:

Getting from the Dining Room to the Bedroom

One of the primary goals in serving your guest a seductive dinner is, frankly, copulation. As in marketing a product (you, in this case) you've got to close the sale, which generally means making an offer. Not that difficult a task, in my experience, once you have plied her with great food, fine wine, strong liquor and piquant conversation. Bear in mind that she would not have accepted your invitation for dîner pour deux at your place—consciously putting herself in a potentially romantic situation—if she had no romantic inclination toward you.

But then, post-prandially, how to get her from the dinner table to the bedroom or other venue conducive to "love"?
(Though I'll note that the dinner table itself has at times served that role marvelously.) Of course a loveseat or divan is
a divine staging area and/or consummation site. It is also a natural and comfortable place to have an after-dinner drink.
Also, it guarantees close physical proximity, where it is easy to signal your desires and intentions with a touch or perhaps
a glance, a breath or an innuendo.

However, I realize that not all men or women are inclined to demonstrate or understand subtlety. And I, for one, have
never been the sort of man to start pawing a woman without an invitation—at least when sober. So at times it is wise and
gentlemanly—and, most important, effective—to be direct and ask permission.

Usually the honest phrase that springs spontaneously and unaffectedly to mind serves best. E.g., "Miss Cramer, you have
a beautiful ass!"

However, if you find yourself at a loss for such words, it is important to have a few stock phrases in store that you can
employ:

"Would you care for a euphemistic back rub?" has worked with English majors and such.

"I'd love to have at you," scores marks for directness and honesty.

And the venerable, "Hey! Let's fuck!"—when delivered with the proper amount of seeming spontaneity, as if the idea
had just suddenly risen from an infinitum of possible activities—often hits the mark.

In this—as in all endeavors—I encourage you to be bold and creative.

Chapter 3

Raw Meat for a Savage Carnivore

Despite the dire warnings from neo-Puritans (more on them later) about eating raw meat and eggs, steak tartare is not likely what's going to get you, and, trust me, something will one day get you.

We take risks every day of our lives: driving on the freeway, biking in the park, walking down dark streets, flying to another city, shaking hands with strangers, sliding into third base, sitting under a coconut palm, and taking drugs, legal or otherwise. Despite the dire warnings from neo-Puritans (more on them later) about eating raw meat and eggs, steak tartare is not likely what's going to get you, and, trust me, something will one day get you. In the meantime I suggest gusto and steak tartare. And the safest place to consume it is at home, where you set and execute the standards for cleanliness.

I have made and consumed steak tartare scores of times over the years without any ill effects. I'll tell you how to do it and create a sensuous and seductive repast in the process—for nothing brings out the savage in a woman like her consuming raw meat. Of course, it is probably best to check when tendering the dinner invitation if she would be amenable to eating some raw meat at your place. You might be pleasantly surprised by her response.

But as to the potential health risks: First, if the rare salmonella in eggs concerns you, simply buy pasteurized eggs. Problem solved. Though, personally, I've never used them, and have enjoyed raw eggs in steak tartare, Caesar salad, eggnog and other dishes without issue.

Likewise for the uncooked beef, I have developed a regimen that produces uniformly safe, healthful and delicious dinners. Read on:

Steak Tartare

Ingredients:

3/4 lb. *filet, sirloin tip, or round steak* or similar lean cut.

1 raw *egg* yolk.

3 tablespoons *extra virgin olive* oil.

Capers.

Dry mustard.

Chopped *scallions or minced shallots.*

Chopped fresh *parsley.*

Anchovies.

Freshly *ground black pepper.*

Coarse sea salt.

Rye or French bread.

Steps:

- Select a fresh lean cut of unground beef. Filet is fine if you can afford it. If not, sirloin or round steak will work. For two people, 3/4 pound ought to do it.

- Run a little cold water on it and wipe it down with a clean kitchen towel.

- Cut the meat into 1.5-inch chunks, using a clean carving knife and cutting board.

- Feed the chunks a couple at a time into your blender or food processor to grind them to hamburger. (Or, if you prefer, simply cut the meat into 1.5-inch chunks.)

- Place the meat at the center of a platter, taking care to shape it attractively—circular or oval shape, perhaps two inches thick. With the carving knife, fashion diamond-shaped crosshatches on the top of the meat.

- Separate a raw egg yolk from the white—this is easily done by cracking the egg in half and passing the yolk back and forth from shell half to shell half, tipping out the white in the process while careful not to cut the yolk on the shell edges.

- With the back of a tablespoon, press a shallow hollow in the center of the ground beef and tip the unbroken yolk into it.

- Pour some good extra virgin olive oil over it—perhaps three tablespoons.

- Arrange the capers, scallions, dry mustard, anchovies, parsley, pepper and coarse sea salt on the perimeter of the platter in separate piles.

As to the bread: I prefer rye toast points. Get a loaf of delicatessen rye with caraway seeds, toast a few thin slices in a clean fry pan, and then cut them into 1-in. by 3-in. triangles. A good French bread, sliced and toasted also works fine.

You can set out Tabasco and Worcestershire sauce if that's to your taste, but I like my tartare largely unadulterated, without sauce or anchovies, savoring the creamy taste of the raw meat and raw egg in olive oil on a slice of rye toast.

A green salad would complement the raw meat nicely.

For wine, I like a lighter red with this, perhaps something from Beaujolais—a Brouilly or Fleurie. Also, why not Champagne? One New Year's Eve I served a vintage French brut with the steak tartare to an accommodating blonde. Actually, that has happened more than once, and always with festive results!

Straight from Bent:

The Advance of the Neo-Puritans

Under the dubious guise of benefitting society and promoting public health and safety, a new breed of secular American Puritans have wormed their way into positions of power and influence. These "well meaning" totalitarians would have us not smoke tobacco or fornicate freely and naturally. They would limit our intake of salt, calories, carbohydrates, raw meat and alcohol. They would happily and puritanically suck all the sensual pleasure from our lives so as to make us as miserable as they are.

They say they do this for our own good or to lower healthcare costs or to keep us from harming others with secondhand smoke. (No mention ever of secondhand stress, which they spread liberally and malevolently, along with great servings of misinformation and outright lies.) Don't believe them and don't give in to their prescriptions and proscriptions.

Just like the early Puritans, these 21st century austerity freaks want to brand and persecute us for the unseemly sin of enjoying life and sensual pleasure. Ironically, many came from the If-It-Feels-Good-Do-It-Generation. (Do not underestimate the motivating power of personal guilt.) I hope you will raise a glass of absinthe with me and toast their demise!

Cheers!

Chapter 4

Rack of Lamb Provençal

I love lamb in many incarnations: a roast leg of lamb with white wine and black olives, lamb kebobs, braised lamb shanks, Greek moussaka, and, perhaps the most elegant and tastiest, roast rack of lamb Provençal.

Straight from Bent:

"What Don't You Eat?"

In these days of food fads it's smart to find out before you plan the menu if she has any culinary kinks— sometimes as surprising as the other kinks you may later discover. So I always ask, "What don't you eat?"

In reply I often hear the common preferences, prohibitions and prejudices: no meat, no veal, no gluten, no carbs, no pork, no salt, no GMO, etc., despite them all being healthful (for most people) and delicious when deftly prepared.

But I've also fielded some unexpected replies, such as, "I don't eat filters" (meaning, I came to learn, anything prepared with liver) and "I eat nothing with four legs," to which I made a salty reply about my bipedal status and earned a saucy smirk. Of course the most welcome response to your culinary query is: "I'll eat anything and everything you got, baby!"

I love lamb in many incarnations: a roast leg of lamb with white wine and black olives, lamb kebobs, braised lamb shanks, Greek moussaka, and, perhaps the most elegant and tastiest, roast rack of lamb Provençal. It's a dish, when done right, that will impress provincials and sophisticates alike. And, a further lure: It's easy to prepare, either on the grill or in the oven.

Rack of Lamb Provençal

Ingredients:

1 *lamb rack*, 1 1/2 to 2 lbs.

4 tablespoons *herbes de Provence*. (You can buy this dried herb mixture in fine supermarkets and gourmet shops. Alternately, you can mix your own. Typically the mixture contains marjoram, thyme, rosemary, savory, oregano, and lavender leaves, though these last are optional, all chopped fine.)

1 tablespoon *finishing salt* (coarse sea salt).

Steps:

- Dry the meat with a paper towel and cut away any excess fat.

- Rub the lamb with the herb mixture.

- On a hot outdoor grill, brown the meat on all sides.

- Stand the rack up and continue cooking at medium heat until done. This could take a half hour for medium rare. Occasionally test for doneness by pressing your finger against the flat, fleshy side of the rack. When it just begins to firm up, it's done. You can also use a meat thermometer. Cook it to 120 degrees for rare, 150 for medium.

- Alternately, you can roast the herbed rack in a 450-degree F. oven.

- Place the cooked lamb rack on a serving platter, sprinkle on the finishing salt, garnish with fresh herbs or parsley. Let it sit for 10 minutes before carving.

- Carve at the table, slicing between the bones to create individual chops.

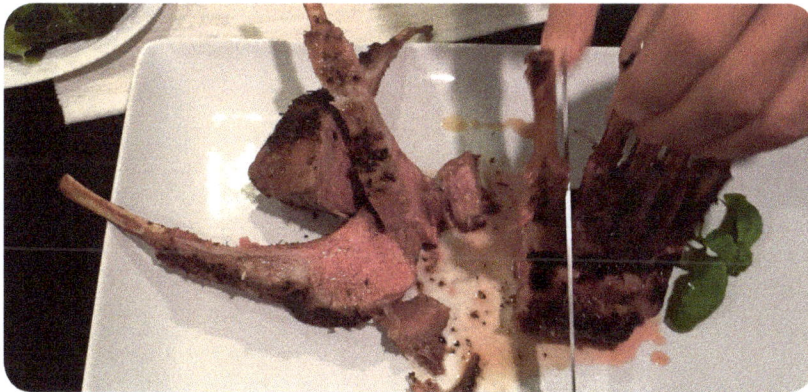

Accompaniments:

Haricots au pistou (*white navy beans—you can also use cannellini beans—with garlic/basil/olive oil sauce*) go well with the lamb. The vibrant green color of the pistou also adds visual interest to the plate. You can simply heat and drain canned beans and add the pistou—which you make by pureeing 1 cup *fresh basil leaves*, 1/2 clove *minced garlic*, salt, and 1/4 cup *extra virgin olive oil* in your blender or food processor. (This is similar to the pesto recipe in Chapter Two, though without the nuts and cheese.)

If using dry beans, soak them overnight and simmer until tender—you can do this ahead of time.

Add to your menu a plain green salad—simply *Boston or Bibb lettuce* with *olive oil* tossed in a garlic-rubbed bowl (no vinegar, which might argue with the wine, but you can add a squeeze of lemon if you prefer) and you have an easy, impressive and elegant meal sure to put your guest in a receptive and suggestible mood.

Some *fresh fruit and cheese* for dessert would complete the meal with a Mediterranean accent.

Wine:

As this is a Mediterranean dish I would serve a hearty red Mediterranean French wine with it: perhaps a Coteaux de Languedoc, a Rhone, or a Cotes de Provence. And don't forget the bottled mineral water.

Straight from Bent:

Getting Her to Leave

Okay, you've followed my instructions: You've created a sexy ambiance, executed a delicious dinner, and successfully seduced the target. (No dehumanizing or misogynistic disrespect meant, ladies, but men understand military metaphors best). However, many women—and this is likely some primitive instinct kicking in—enjoy lying abed post-coitally with a man and perhaps waking to him in the morning. Maybe it's marking turf, maybe it makes her feel secure, maybe she has roommates who rise to alarm clocks, or maybe she actually likes you and your scent. Or maybe she wants to screw all night or start the next day with a bang. Or, on a different practical level, she doesn't want to drive home after wine and Cognac and risk a ticket or worse.

But now, however, for whatever reason, you want to enjoy your solitude. And that reason could be one of many: Perhaps the sex wasn't all that good and you're having second thoughts about the whole affair—sometimes you just don't know until you try each other on for size. Or maybe you're a light sleeper. Or maybe you don't want to see her in the morning when she will not be at her best (and vice versa) and taint retrospectively the romantic moments of the previous night. Or maybe you don't want your neighbors seeing her leave in the morning—though I always say it pays to advertise. Or maybe you have a late date with someone else, or your steady girlfriend just left a message to check on you, to which you need to respond in private. Whatever.

As in most things, I counsel honesty—except when prevarication better suits your purpose. On the other hand, I know that most guys don't like to have to explain themselves and their motives, which are sometimes opaque even to ourselves. Still, you want to get her out the door without hurting her feelings or your chances for an encore at a later date. Perhaps something along these lines might work:

"I'd like to invite you to spend the night, but perhaps next time. I've got some work to do in the morning, and I'm afraid I wouldn't be very good company."

No lie there. I'm sure I wouldn't be good company waking to someone I wish wasn't there! If she gets pissed off at that or turns grumpy, just as well: You've weeded out someone with other than a sweet disposition and who is not sympathetic and deferential to your needs.

But if you are the devious type who enjoys subterfuge, you can have arranged for a friend to call at a certain time, claiming to need your help with a flat tire or whatever. Or you can say you work the night shift. Or tell her that your PTSD causes you to wake screaming on the hour. Or say you have to get up early for the rugby tournament, and that having her in bed all night would be a great distraction, since you'd want to fuck her a few more times and likely not get any sleep, which would wreck your game. If she is not flattered and amused by that—and naughty enough to want a reprise at a later date—better that the unfeeling woman leave in a huff and end things before they go too far.

Chapter 5

Steak Pommes Frites

As simple as it is to prepare, grilled steak and pommes frites, French fries, never fail to please devoted meat- and potato-eaters. Additionally, when served with a nice Bordeaux or Burgundy, they conjure up Paris and romance, which can lead to additional pleasures.

As noted, a French wine would add atmosphere to the meal. But also a big Argentine Carménère or an Italian Super Tuscan would go great with this simple yet elegant fare.

I prefer to cook the meat in a cast-iron skillet for uniform doneness and seared exterior, and use the cold-oil method for the frites, a ploy favored by noted chefs.

Beef Steak with Butter

Ingredients:

2 *steaks*, 1/2 to 1 lb. each. Thick rib eye or filet are my first choices.

Freshly *ground black pepper.*

3 tablespoons *unsalted butter,* softened.

1 teaspoon finely chopped *fresh thyme* leaves.

1 *clove garlic,* minced or processed through a garlic press.

1 tablespoon *lemon juice.*

Coarse sea salt.

Steps:

- Prepare the steak butter ahead of time if you wish. Simply combine the softened butter, thyme, black pepper, garlic, and lemon juice. Refrigerate.

- Heat the skillet on a hot burner, as hot as you can get it, and add the steaks.

- Sear and cook the steaks on one side, without turning, for perhaps 3 minutes for 1-inch thick steaks. Turn and cook until done, perhaps just another minute or two, testing frequently for doneness. For medium rare, which I prefer, the steaks should feel somewhat springy to the touch, not unlike the heel of your outstretched thumb when prodded with your forefinger.

- Remove the steaks to two dinner plates and top with the steak butter and sea salt.

- Garnish with fresh thyme sprigs.

French Fries

Ingredients:

1 large *russet potato,* sliced into narrow fries, 1/4 inch thick.

Peanut oil.

Salt.

You can cut the fries before cooking the steaks and have them waiting in the oil to cook quickly after you finish the steaks, which will improve if you let them rest for the five or ten minutes it takes you to fry the potatoes. I use the cold-oil method for crisp and succulent pommes frites.

Steps:

- Pour peanut oil into a large, cold skillet to 1/2 inch depth.

- Add the potatoes to the cold oil.

- Turn the heat to high.

- Cook the potatoes without turning (though watchful to keep them separate and not sticking together) until the undersides begin to brown. Only then should you turn them.

- Continue to cook and turn until uniformly light brown.

- Remove from the skillet with a slotted spoon and drain in a colander.

- Arrange the fries on the dinner plates alongside the steaks.

A green salad—Bibb, Boston, or red leaf lettuce—would be a perfect accompaniment. Simply wash and dry the lettuce, rub a salad bowl with a garlic half, and toss the lettuce there with extra virgin olive oil, salt and pepper.

Chapter 6

Cock with Wine (Coq au Vin)

An easy-to-prepare, seductive and relatively foolproof dinner for the fledgling chef, cock with wine (coq au vin, in French) weds chicken, bacon, onions and red wine in a dish designed to get the digestive juices, among others, flowing.

Straight from Bent:

Business Cards as a Means to Bliss

Yeah, I know that business cards are so 20th century and kill innocent trees et cetera, but every man should still carry some, as they can lead to unexpected pleasure.

A simple card with name, phone number and email address can pay great dividends, for they can be handed over or slipped into purses or blouse pockets quickly and casually. At times you'll meet women who are otherwise engaged—with friends, on a date with another man or her husband, or on a plane—whom you find interesting but whom you don't have the time or opportunity to charm right then. In such cases I hand the woman my card and tell her to call anytime. Often she will reciprocate with her card—and often call when you least expect it, which is always a delightful surprise.

I never put a title or profession on my card—in part because I have never held a job, earned a degree or joined a club, and have casual credentials in so many endeavors. Not infrequently a woman will study my card and ask, "What is it you do?" That gives me the opportunity to reply wittily and extemporaneously to suit the occasion, or to retrieve one of my ready-made replies:

"What is it you need done?"

Or, "I'm a talent scout."

Or, simply, honestly and mysteriously, "Research."

The bottom line is that every now and then I'll get a call from someone whom I can't remember, but who wants to come to dinner. It's like the grab bag at the county fair when you were a child: always intriguing, occasionally exhilarating, at times disappointing, but always worth a dime for the thrill.

Coq au Vin

Ingredients:

1/8 lb. *thick-sliced bacon* (2 strips) cut into 1/4-inch by 1-inch lardons.

1 tablespoon *olive oil.*

1 *small chicken,* quartered, or 4 leg quarters (my preference, as dark meat remains juicier in chicken stews, though your date may prefer white meat).

1/4 cup *flour.*

1/4 cup *brandy.*

Salt and freshly ground black pepper.

1 *bay leaf.*

1/4 teaspoon *dried thyme.*

12 *small white onions*, peeled. (You can ease peeling but dropping the onions in boiling water for 2 minutes.)

1 cup *dry red wine.*

1 cup *chicken bouillon.*

1 *garlic clove,* smashed.

2 tablespoons *chili sauce or catsup* (Most coq au vin recipes suggest tomato paste, but these work just as well, and you don't have to open a whole can of tomato paste, whose remaining contents will turn brown in the fridge.)

1/2 pound *fresh mushrooms,* quartered.

1 tablespoon *unsalted butter.*

Parsley or fresh thyme sprigs for garnish.

Steps:

- In a heavy skillet or Dutch oven, brown the bacon in the olive oil over medium heat and set the bacon aside.

- Dust the chicken pieces with flour and brown them lightly on all sides in the olive oil and bacon grease over medium heat.

- Add the brandy, let it heat till it begins steaming then ignite it with a match, careful not to set yourself or the kitchen afire. This will burn off the alcohol in a few seconds. If you feel the need to kill the fire, put a lid on it.

- Season the chicken with salt and pepper.

- Add the bay leaf, thyme, onions, garlic clove, and cooked bacon.

- Pour in the wine, chicken bouillon and catsup.

- Cover and simmer for 30 minutes. (Check the chicken and onions for doneness. If the onions need to cook longer, remove the chicken and continue simmering until ready. The only way you can mess this dish up is by overcooking the chicken. You can check that by removing a piece and placing it on a white plate to see if juices run clear or bloody. If the latter, cook it a bit longer.)

- While the chicken is simmering, sauté the mushrooms in the butter over medium high heat.

- The wine sauce should be the consistency of a thin gravy. If it is not thick enough, remove the chicken and onions from the pan and boil it till it thickens a bit.

- Skim off excessive fat.

- Add the sautéed mushrooms and simmer for two minutes.

- Serve on dinner plates, one piece of chicken per plate, along with the onions, mushrooms and sauce. Garnish with the parsley or fresh thyme.

Also you can make this dish ahead of time and even refrigerate it overnight. Just be sure to warm it slowly over low heat so as not to overcook the bird. A green salad and a loaf of French bread, along with a bottle of Cotes du Rhone or pinot noir, make for perfect accompaniments. Or, if you'd like to add some more color, try one of my favorite, easy-to-make veggies, Carrots Vichy:

Carrots Vichy

Ingredients:

1 lb. *whole carrots.*

2 tablespoons *unsalted butter.*

1/4 cup *water.*

1/2 teaspoon *sugar.*

1/4 cup *chopped fresh parsley.*

Salt and freshly ground pepper.

Steps:

- Peel and cut the carrots into 3-inch long, 1/2-inch thick spears.

- Heat the water, butter and sugar to boiling in a saucepan.

- Add the carrots and cook vigorously until carrots are not quite done, that is, when they still offer some resistance when pierced with a dinner fork.

- Remove the carrots and boil away any remaining water.

- Lower the heat to medium and return the carrots to the pot, browning and searing the carrots in the remaining butter. Remove from the heat and toss with the parsley, salt and pepper.

Straight from Bent:

What if She Invites YOU to Dinner at Her Place?

If she tenders you an intimate dinner invitation, that's usually a positive sign, at least on one level, as it means she is likely trying to seduce you.

However enticing and flattering that may be, bear in mind that by accepting her invitation you run the risk of being served mediocre fare. Just hope she's read this book. If not, pray for the best but be prepared for the worst.

Over the years I have forced down a number of excremental meals and indifferent bottles of wine at bachelorette pads. And a bad meal, for me, can take the glow off the evening, even if she serves up some delicious booty for dessert. If so, and she merits an encore, reciprocate by having her to dinner at your place, knowing that you will both eat, drink and fuck well. It's a win-win for all concerned.

Chapter 7

Grilled Salmon with Zest, Couscous and Asparagus Vinaigrette

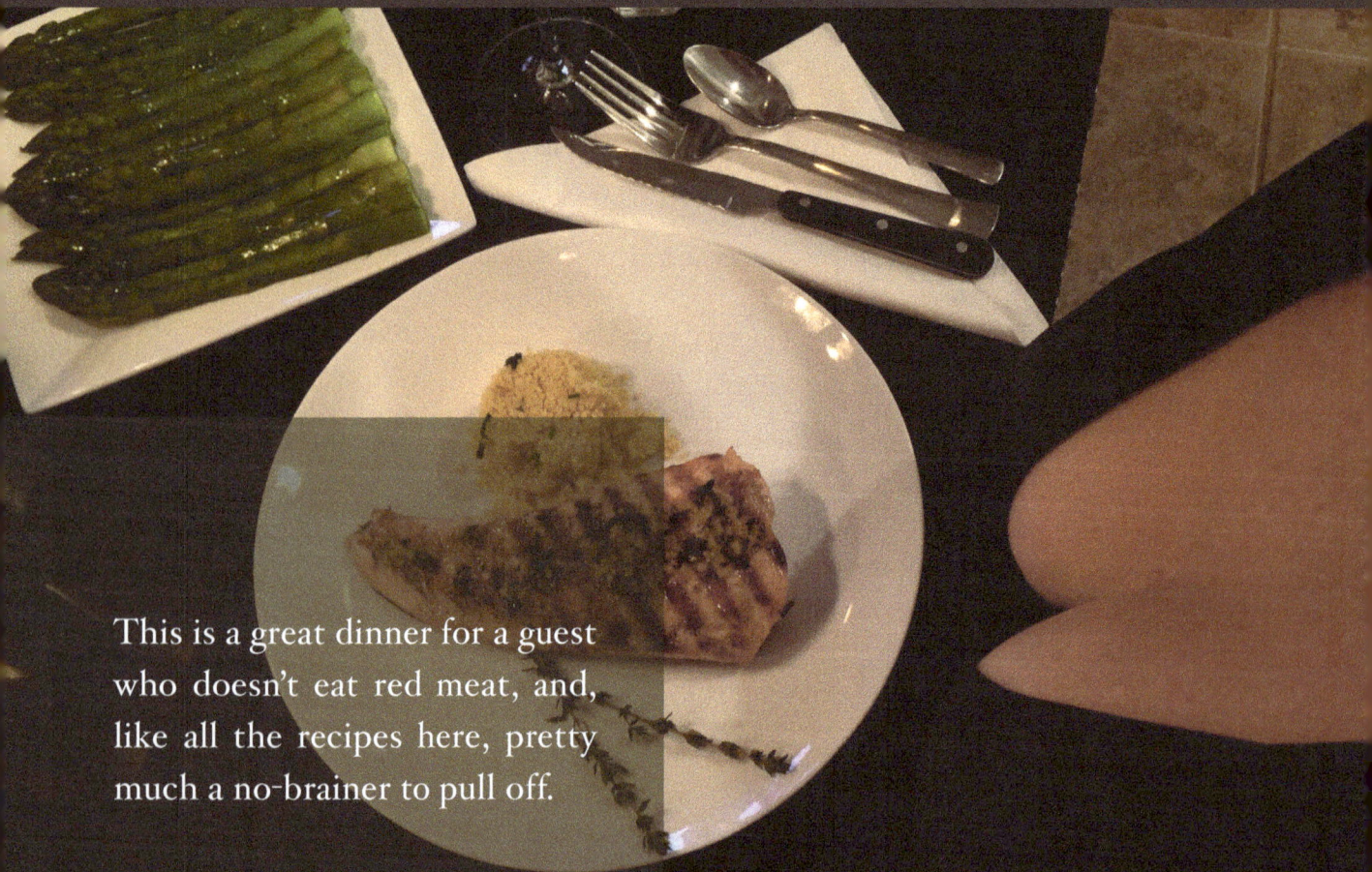

This is a great dinner for a guest who doesn't eat red meat, and, like all the recipes here, pretty much a no-brainer to pull off.

This is a great dinner for a guest who doesn't eat red meat, and, like all the recipes here, pretty much a no-brainer to pull off. Also, salmon—either the wild-caught or the farm-raised—is inexpensive and delicious if you take care not to overcook it like most people do. It should be crispy on the outside and, to my taste, rare on the inside. To accomplish that you need a super-hot grill or grill pan.

Also, since you are a one-man-band without competent kitchen help, you always need to orchestrate the cooking so that everything is done at the right time and served at the right temperature—which is easy for this menu. Make the asparagus first or ahead of time; concoct the lemon zest sauce for the salmon; heat the grill; make the couscous, keeping it covered and warm; grill the salmon, which should take only five or ten minutes.

As to wine, I like a crisp, dry French white chardonnay from Burgundy to stand up to the piquant grilled fish and couscous. A dry rosé would also work.

Salmon with Lemon Zest

Ingredients:

2 pieces *salmon*, approx. 1 lb. total. (I prefer steaks, which are thicker and juicier; however, filets are fine as well.)

1 *lemon*.

1 clove *garlic,* pressed.

1 tablespoon finely chopped *fresh thyme*.

3 tablespoons *extra virgin olive oil*.

Salt and freshly ground pepper.

Steps:

- Using your cheese grater, grate all *the yellow skin* from a lemon into a small mixing bowl, careful not to grate in any of the bitter white rind.

- Add the garlic clove that has been run through your garlic press (or chopped fine), the chopped thyme, salt, pepper, and olive oil. Stir.

- Grill the salmon on high heat after oiling the grill or grill pan so that the fish won't stick to the grill. If using fillets with skin on one side, cook flesh-side down for a few minutes, turning only after the meat is nearly done.

- To test for doneness, press on the filet or steak with your fingertip. It should feel a bit springy in the center. If it feels firm, you've overcooked it. And since salmon flakes nicely, you can also use a steak knife to poke and peer inside. It should still appear darker in the center, not uniformly pink, which indicates overcooked meat. And don't forget that it will continue to cook even after you take it from the grill.

Arrange the grilled salmon on dinner plates, top with the lemon zest sauce, and garnish with thyme sprigs and lemon slices.

Curried Couscous

Couscous—the traditional North African granulated semolina pasta—is a quick, easy, and delicious accompaniment to the salmon. (It also goes well with camel meat, as I can attest from my days among the Bedouin.) Further, it is readily available in the rice/pasta aisle of most supermarkets.

You can flavor it in many ways, though I generally make it very simply, usually just with sautéed garlic, olive oil and parsley or thyme. But since those ingredients are used in our lemon-zest salmon, we'll want to vary tastes here. The curry adds not only piquancy to the meal but also an appealing visual contrast to the pink salmon and the green asparagus.

Ingredients:

2 tablespoons finely chopped *scallions* (that is, green onion).

1 tablespoon *olive oil.*

1/2 teaspoon *curry powder.*

1/2 cup *water.*

Salt, just a pinch or two.

1/2 cup *couscous.*

Steps:

- Sauté the scallions in the olive oil.

- Add the curry powder and stir.

- Add the water and salt and bring to a boil.

- Add the couscous, stir, remove from the heat, and cover.

- Let sit for five minutes. It will keep warm for much longer if necessary.

- When done, stir with a fork to separate the granules.

- You can serve molded via a small bowl or measuring cup.

Asparagus Vinaigrette

This cold or room temperature (my preference) dish can be made ahead of time. It is simple to accomplish—as long as you don't overcook the asparagus.

Ingredients:

1/2 to 1/3 lb. fresh *asparagus spears.*

2 tablespoons *white wine vinegar.*

1 teaspoon *Dijon mustard.*

1 teaspoon finely chopped *fresh parsley.*

Salt and pepper.

4 tablespoons *extra virgin olive oil.*

Steps:

- Wash the asparagus and cut off the hard stems—usually an inch or so at the bottom.

- Place the asparagus in a vegetable steamer with water, cover, and bring the water to a boil.

- Check the asparagus frequently to avoid overcooking. Once the water starts boiling, this should take only a few minutes. Using a sharp dinner fork, test a stem: When it pierces it with just a modicum of resistance, it's done.

- Remove the asparagus and plunge into cold water briefly—perhaps just half a minute—to halt the cooking. Drain and dry.

- Add the vinegar, olive oil, parsley, salt and pepper to a small bowl and mix thoroughly with a whisk.

- Toss the asparagus with the mixture and serve neatly arranged on side plates.

Straight from Bent:

How Does a Lady Eat Asparagus?

How your dinner guest consumes her asparagus can give you a glimpse into her psyche and perhaps serve as a conversational icebreaker.

If she picks up a spear with her fingers and slides it tip-first sensuously between her pouty lips—perhaps even licking it—this is a good sign of promised pleasure. It also serves as an opportunity to comment on her technique, bringing it to her attention if it had been done subconsciously, and directing the dinner conversation into more productive if not reproductive areas.

However, if she chops the asparagus tips off with her knife and them skewers them with her fork, watch out!, for this could indicate certain castration fantasies—though most likely aimed at her husband or an ex-beau. Or it could mean that she just loves asparagus tips!

Chapter 8

Le Diner Impromptu á la Walgreens

Even if you are not well-stocked or are perhaps away from home in a vacation cottage or condo, tantalizing options remain.

Opportunities for pleasure can arise without warning: You find a woman warming to you at a club; you get a late night call from someone you slipped your business card to weeks earlier (see my aside on business cards, above); the stewardess on your flight home has a layover, as they say.

Though my inborn aversion to institutions and group action prohibited me from ever becoming a Boy Scout, I've always taken to heart their motto, "Be Prepared." Which is why I have a cupboard stocked with non-perishables such as good pasta, anchovies, and Italian canned tomatoes—as well as wine and liquor—that can be orchestrated into a romantic dinner in minutes.

However, even if you are not well-stocked or are perhaps away from home in a vacation cottage or condo, tantalizing options remain, as I discovered one humid night in Key West, where I had come to visit my aforementioned Navy pilot nephew, as well as for the diving—of whatever sort.

On the dive boat one December afternoon I met two French Canadian women vacationers, both in their late 20s—one of which, Anne Marie, was buff (bikinis tell no lies) and ravishing; the other, Giselle, mousey. I suggested a drink at a pier-side bar. After a couple mojitos I invited them both to dinner at my rented vacation studio, whose kitchen was well equipped but whose cupboard was bare.

Good girlfriends, I've learned, communicate with each other better than any married couple. (Not to mention somehow synching their periods.) This evening I now noted their eyes meeting and a tacit understanding being reached.

Anne Marie turned to me. "Merci. I should like zat zo very much."

Giselle, however, claiming to be too exhausted from a day on the water to be good company, demurred. I feigned disappointment, mildly, thinking to myself, "Le gran prix!"

I gave Anne Marie directions to my condo on the Atlantic.

But I had arrived in Key West just the night before and had nothing there to eat. Further, she told me she did not eat meat—I presumed she meant the dead variety. And the one grocery in downtown Key West was just locking its doors as I approached. But I knew there was a Walgreens just a block away—and knew from experience that in emergencies the resourceful and knowledgeable roué can extemporize a romantic meal from its meager food market.

Here's what I found on Walgreens' shelves and in its coolers and carried back to my rented condo: Spanish olives, unsalted butter, eggs, Swiss cheese, chocolate ice cream, garlic powder, onion powder, salt, pepper, red pepper flakes, dried oregano, sesame breadsticks, organic Italian penne pasta, canned diced tomatoes, a white Bordeaux, a bottle of Beaujolais, a pint of Cognac, a bottle of Perrier, and scentless candles. Voila!

Anne Marie arrived transformed from mermaid to chic cosmopolitan in a crinkly white dress and wedgies as the sun was setting over the Dry Tortugas. We watched its exit from my balcony, sipping the white Bordeaux and nibbling on the Spanish olives (topped with olive oil and oregano) as the sky turned pink, red and Gulf Stream blue.

I led her to the small kitchen with breakfast bar. She took a barstool and crossed her legs, the dress riding up nicely to reveal the taut thighs I had glimpsed on the dive boat. But here they were even more inviting, what with the catch-me-fuck-me shoes and the sultry dark brown hair now falling to her shoulders.

She watched with interest as I broke five eggs into a bowl, mixed them with a fork, added shredded Swiss cheese, salt, and pepper, then sizzled a generous cube of butter in a skillet. I sluiced the eggs into the hot butter, and practiced benign indifference for a minute or two as the eggs began to congeal and the cheese to melt. But before the eggs had cooked fully, I used a flipper to double the omelet over, and slid it from the skillet to a serving platter, where I garnished the dish with a couple palm fronds that I had liberated from a plant in the patio below.

We sat at the breakfast bar, where I had lit two candles and placed the breadsticks in a tumbler. We touched wine glasses, toasting to pleasure, and devoured the buttery omelet and breadsticks, washed down with Perrier and the white wine.

Next, for the main course, I put water on the boil, adding two fistfuls of salt, and sautéed the diced tomatoes in olive oil with salt, red pepper, oregano, garlic powder and onion powder, leaving the lid off the saucepan so the sauce would thicken and the aromas would season the air.

A Hot Interlude

Serendipity often plays an important part in pleasure—perhaps a large part. So you must always be prepared to improvise and avoid rigid plans—particularly when other, more pressing things rigidify. Such was the case that night.

While we waited for the pasta water to boil I complimented Anne Marie on her fitness. Playfully, she flexed her biceps so I could feel her muscle. I did so then ran my hands down her sides to her buttocks.

"Firm there too?" I asked.

She smirked, rose from her barstool, turned and placed her hands on the breakfast bar. And I then...Ah, je me souviens, as they say in Quebec.

Next Course

That intermezzo worked to build a great appetite in us both. The tomato sauce was perking and the water was boiling away. I dumped the pasta into it and stirred. Now I gave my focused attention to the new job at hand.

The bad meals and mishaps that most amateur cooks concoct come from negligence. You can't cook from the living room or while you're bullshitting the guests or otherwise distracted. And it even happens to professional chefs when they are trying to do four things at once. Inattention at a key moment can ruin a steak through overcooking or produce unappetizing flaccid pasta and ruin a meal, perhaps breaking the romantic spell and robbing you of the ultimate pleasure.

Even though Anne Marie and I had already shared that ultimate pleasure, I wanted more, as well as a savory dinner to satisfy just as well our other hunger. So after a couple minutes I began testing the pasta's consistency every 30 seconds, using a slotted spoon to retrieve a piece for tasting. The key is to get the pasta quickly out of the water before it is done cooking—for it will continue to cook once removed from the water. Pasta should be firm, al dente, as the Italians say. Which means it should still be a little doughy and crisp when you dump it and the water out into the waiting colander, where it will drain. Timing this may take a bit of practice and experience. I say practice on yourself—cooking pasta, that is—so you can duly impress your guest when the time comes to perform.

By this time Anne Marie and I were already into the Beaujolais—always one of my favorite light red wines: consistently good, inexpensive, and just fine with tomato sauce.

With the pasta done perfectly, I spooned generous portions onto two plates and topped it with a modicum of the fragrant tomato sauce—not too much, for you want to taste the pasta, and not have it swimming in sauce. I drizzled more olive oil on top. She loved it, never guessing it came from the drug store.

Yet Another Interlude

Sated—but only in gustatory way—we settled on the love seat facing the balcony, glimpsing above the sparkling Atlantic a dark blue sky littered with thousands of stars. We toasted again, this time with snifters of brandy.

I've always preferred loveseats to beds as sexual venues, as they present so many more positioning opportunities—as Anne Marie and I now demonstrated. But this is a cookbook, not the *Kama Sutra*, so I won't bore you with the variations. However, if you wish to take a moment of silence to imagine them, please do so...

Now back to dessert.

The Final Course

The chocolate ice cream—a good brand, with real cream—awaited us in the freezer. But to elevate it and create an elegant end to the meal and the evening, I had decided on some pyrotechnics.

I spooned small portions of the ice cream into petite bowls then heated a half cup of brandy in a saucepan. When it began to steam I touched a lit match to the Cognac, careful to keep my distance and my face turned away as it burst into flame. When the alcohol burned off I poured the flambé over the chocolate ice cream. This we ate as we sat on the balcony, contemplating how sweet life is.

As she finished her dessert, Anne Marie apologized:

"I am zo zorry, Bentley, but I cannot sleep here wiz you. I have promised Giselle I would be home tonight as we have ze early boat for ze Dry Tortugas tomorrow morning."

Ah, the perfect ending to a perfect night! I could get a good night's sleep without a stranger sprawled beside me, and wake refreshed with my own thoughts, my own sweet memories and my own routines. I said I was sorry as well, and was about to bid her au revoir when a thought suddenly occurred to me:

"Hey! On va baiser!"

Les Hors D'ourves

Ingredients:

- *Spanish olives,* room temp.

- *Dried oregano.*

- *Extra virgin olive oil.*

- *White Bordeaux* wine, chilled.

Steps:

- Arrange the olives on a small plate or saucer.

- Drizzle olive oil over them.

- Sprinkle the olives with dried oregano.

Open the chilled wine, pour into white wine glasses (which are narrower than red wine glasses, to help keep it cool) and toast her beauty.

Keep the wine nearby, on ice, so it's easy to pour more and keep things flowing.

Le Omelet

Ingredients:

Unsalted butter, a goodly chunk—2 or 3 tablespoons.

Five eggs.

A *couple slices of Swiss cheese* (or whatever looks best and costs most in the Walgreens cheese department. But never, ever buy grated "Parmesan" in a cardboard shaker, the stuff that smells as if regurgitated.)

Salt and pepper.

Sesame, garlic or other *breadsticks.*

Steps:

- Break the eggs into a bowl; stir with a fork.

- Cut the Swiss cheese in one-inch long strips; add to the eggs.

- Season with salt and pepper.

- Apply medium high heat to an iron or steel skillet; add the butter; when it is sizzling, pour in the egg mixture.

- Just watch it cook. Don't mess with it. After a minute or two, when the top is still barely uncooked, fold the omelet in half. It should be browned nicely by now.

- Slide it on to a serving platter and garnish with whatever you might have at hand.

- At the table cut it in half and serve her the larger piece.

- To be accompanied by the breadsticks and white wine.

Pasta with Tomato Sauce

Ingredients:

- 1 16-oz. can *diced Roma tomatoes.*

- 1/4 teaspoon *garlic powder.*

- 1/4 teaspoon *onion powder.*

- 1/4 teaspoon *red pepper flakes.*

- 1 teaspoon *dried oregano.*

- 1/4 cup *extra virgin olive oil.*

- *Salt.*

- 12 oz. *organic Italian penne pasta.*

Steps:

- Mix the tomatoes, garlic powder, onion powder, red pepper, oregano and olive oil in a cooking pot.

- Cook the mixture at medium high heat for 15 minutes, or until the sauce acquires a thick, creamy consistency.

- Heat 2 gallons of water to boiling in a two-handled pot.

- Add 1/4 cup salt to the boiling water.

- Add the pasta and stir. Boil while stirring occasionally. After a few minutes, retrieve a piece from the water to test for doneness. You want to take it out before it is fully cooked, while still just a bit hard in the center, as it will continue to cook out of the water.

- In the sink, pour out the contents in a colander. Shake to remove excess water.

- In a large mixing bowl, stir together half the tomato sauce with the pasta.

- Arrange on individual dinner plates in modest portions—1/4 lb. is sufficient. Spoon two tablespoons of the tomato sauce in the center of the serving. Garnish with whatever is handy— in this case I used some magenta bougainvillea that was entwining around the balcony, and also offered Anne Marie a flower, which she fixed above her ear. Perfect.

Ice Cream with Cognac Flambé

Ingredients:

1/2 pint *ice cream*.

1/2 cup *Cognac or brandy*.

(**Optional:** If you wish to add fresh fruit such as *blueberries or raspberries*—always a nice touch—you can do so at Step One, along with a tablespoon of *sugar* and a tablespoon of *cornstarch*.)

Steps:

- Heat the brandy in a saucepan over medium heat.

- When it begins to steam, remove it from the heat and touch the surface with a long match or lighter, careful not to ignite you or your surroundings.

- Allow for most of the alcohol to burn off. This could take half a minute.

- Cover the pan to extinguish the flames.

- Pour over the ice cream portions and serve.

Chapter 9

Some Recommended Cookbooks

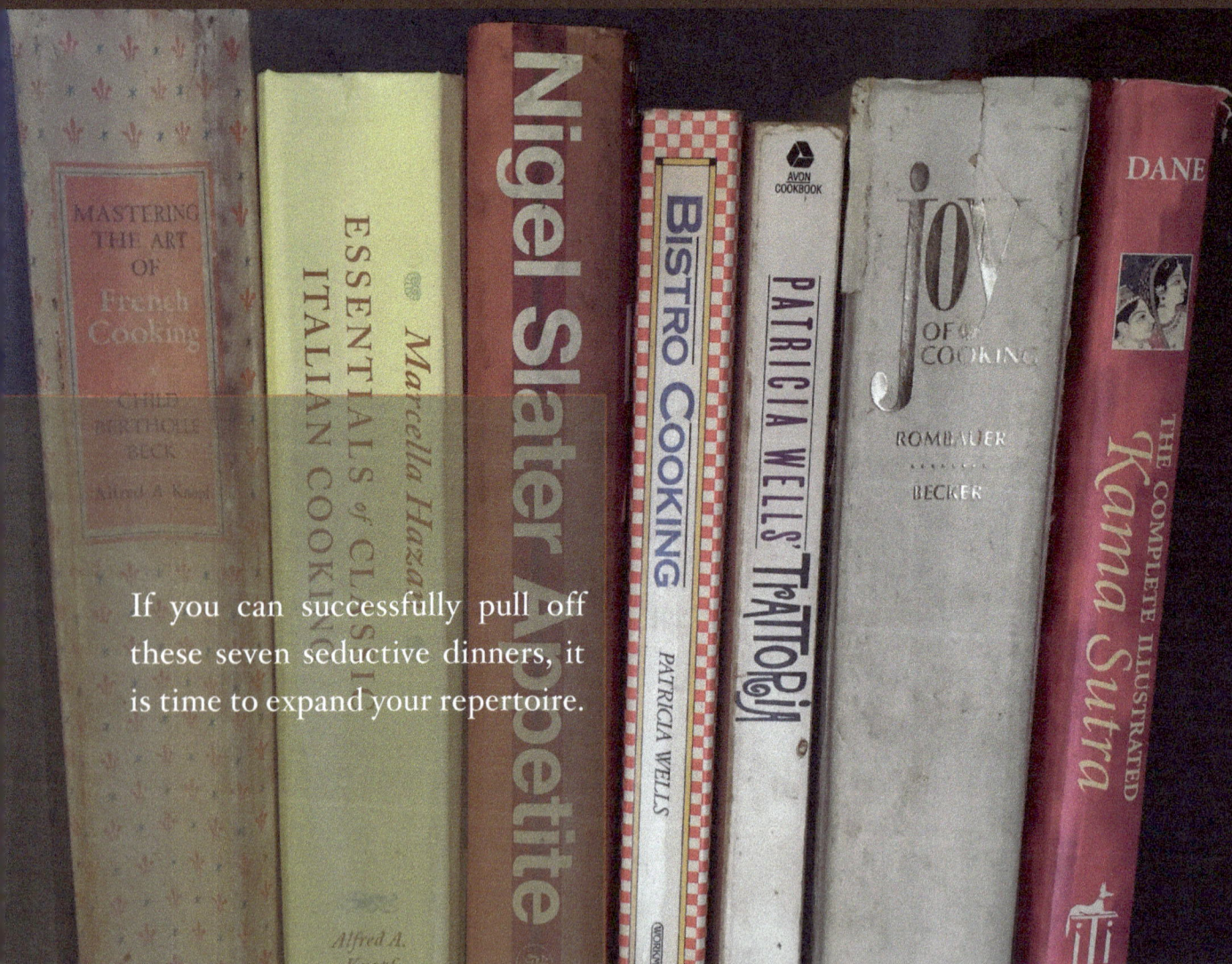

If you can successfully pull off these seven seductive dinners, it is time to expand your repertoire.

MASTERING THE ART OF French Cooking

CHILD BERTHOLLE BECK

Alfred A. Knopf

ESSENTIALS of CLASSIC ITALIAN COOKING

Marcella Hazan

Nigel Slater Appetite

BISTRO COOKING

PATRICIA WELLS

PATRICIA WELLS' TRATTORIA

AVON COOKBOOK

JOY OF COOKING

ROMBAUER

BECKER

DANE

THE COMPLETE ILLUSTRATED Kama Sutra

Alfred A. Knopf

-*Mastering the Art of French Cooking,* Volume I, by Julia Child, Louisette Bertholle and Simon Beck. The bible for French cooking, with great recipes for traditional French fare. Many of the recipes are labor-intensive but always worth the effort. The fricassee de poulet a l'ancienne—old-fashioned chicken fricassee with wine-flavored cream sauce, onions and mushrooms—delivers the best chicken dish ever. Also try the boeuf à la mode and the daube à la Provençal.

-*Essentials of Classic Italian Cooking,* by Marcella Hazan. Hazan is to Italian cooking what Julia Child is to French cooking—a go-to popularizing authority on traditional fare. Great and surprising pasta dishes—such as the scallop sauce with olive oil, garlic, and hot pepper, topped with, of all things, toasted breadcrumbs. Kudos also for the grilled fish Romagna style, veal scallopine with lemon, creative vegetable dishes and killer pizza recipes—far better than anything you can have delivered, and not that difficult to prepare.

-*Everyday French Cooking,* by Henri-Paul Pellaprat. Apparently out of print, but a valuable guide, if you can find it, to the way French fare is—or, perhaps, was—cooked at home in France. Good sections on menu planning and wine.

~*Appetite*, by Nigel Slater. The Brit Slater serves up simple comfort food that excels. Great recipes for roast chicken, baked fish and roast lamb. Not for those concerned about fat, salt and calorie intake but perfect for those devoted to pleasure.

~*Bistro Cooking*, by Patricia Wells. Savory and sometimes surprising French recipes taken from small bistros and homes across France, with creative potato and vegetable dishes along with old-time seafood and meat concoctions.

~*Patricia Wells' Trattoria: Simple and Robust Fare Inspired by the Small Family Restaurants of Italy*, by Patricia Wells and Steven Rothfeld. The title says it all: easy-to-prepare yet fantastic Italian soups, pastas, meats and more.

~*Cucina Rustica: Simple, Irresistible Recipes in the Rustic Italian Style*, by Viana La Place and Evan Kleiman. Another down-to-earth book on traditional Italian cooking. Pasta with uncooked tomato sauce is one recipe I have returned to with delight time and again over the years.

~*Joy of Cooking*, by Irma S. Rombauer, Marion Rombauer Becker and Ethan Becker. A great resource for the basics of cooking and traditional American fare. Also a handy reference for kitchen and cooking basics.

About Bent Tines

Bentley (Bent) Tines, man of intrigue and bon vivant international, has enjoyed food, drink, and women on seven continents. A crack shot, mountain climber, free diver, squash player, literary critic, and chess master, he has wined and dined princesses and prima donnas and served as an advisor to top government officials globally across a range of fascinating topics. A limbo-dancing enthusiast who speaks five languages, he has never held a job, married, voted, joined a club, or graduated, devoting himself primarily to pleasure.

Check out the blog @ BentTines.com for more.

Follow me @BentTines on Twitter.

On Facebook @ Bentley Tines
Become a fan @ facebook.com/I-Never-Got-Laid-In-A-Restaurant

If you find this book to be the sort others may want to own,
consider posting a review to Amazon or GoodReads,
or put it anywhere you please.

Cheers,

Bentley Tines

Shopping Lists

In addition to stocking the hardware in your kitchen, you'll need to stock the pantry. Because the business of seduction should be relatively painless, we've compiled shopping lists for each dinner. Snap a picture (or tear it from this book) and take it along, making it oh so simple.

#1 Spinach Linguine with Pesto

1. *Basil leaves.* (At least enough to make 2 cups, e.g., two or more small packs or bag.)

2. Two large *garlic cloves.* (What you don't use you can keep for later.)

3. *Cherry tomatoes.*

4. *Bag of salad greens.*

5. *Pine nuts.* (A small package, usually found in the nut or produce section. Walnuts may be substituted.)

6. *Extra virgin olive oil.* (Get a big bottle, or can, of good stuff. This is a staple you'll use frequently.)

7. *Salt* and freshly ground *pepper.* (Buy peppercorns, because you want to grind it fresh. If you don't have a pepper mill, buy the jar with a mill on top.)

8. *Parmesan cheese.* (Preferably from Italy, the Parmigiano-Reggiano. Domestic Parmesan can be successfully substituted. Get a good hunk. It keeps in refrigerator.)

9. 1 lb. *spinach linguine.* (DeCecco or other high quality brand.)

10. *Burgundy wine.*

11. *Bottled mineral water.*

12. *Ice cream.* (Vanilla or vanilla/choco mix.)

#2 Steak Tartare

1. 3/4 lb. *filet, sirloin tip,* or *round steak* or similar lean cut.

2. *Eggs.*

3. *Extra virgin olive oil.*

4. *Capers.* (In the pickle/olive aisle.)

5. *Dry mustard.*

6. Freshly *ground black pepper.*

7. *Coarse sea salt.*

8. *Bibb or Green Lettuce.* (The bag stuff works.)

9. *Scallions* or *shallots.*

10. *Fresh parsley bunch.*

11. *Anchovies.* (Canned meat section - next to tuna.)

12. *Rye or French bread.*

13. *Beaujolais wine or Champagne.*

14. *Bottled mineral water.*

#3 Rack of Lamb Provençal

1. 1 *lamb rack*. (Often found vacuum packed in the meat case.)

2. *Herbes de Provence*. (You can buy this dried herb mixture in fine supermarkets and gourmet shops. Alternately, you can mix your own. Typically the mixture contains marjoram, thyme, rosemary, savory, oregano, and lavender leaves, though these last are optional, all chopped fine.)

3. *Finishing salt*. (Coarse sea salt).

4. *Cannellini or Navy beans*. (One can.)

5. *Extra Virgin olive oil*.

6. *Fresh basil*.

7. *Garlic cloves*.

8. *Boston or Bibb lettuce*. (All green lettuce in a bag works.)

9. *Fresh fruit*. (Grapes, raspberries, pear...)

10. *Cheese*. (Brie, Manchego, or other rich cheese.)

11. *Hearty Mediterranean French wine*. (Coteaux de Languedoc, Rhone or Cotes de Provence.)

12. *Bottled mineral water*.

#4 Steak and French Fries

1. *2 steaks*, 1/2 to 1 lb. each. Thick rib eye or filet are my first choices.

2. *Peppercorns* for freshly *ground black pepper.*

3. *Coarse sea salt.*

4. *Regular salt.*

5. *Unsalted butter.*

6. *Peanut oil.*

7. *Bibb, Boston or red leaf lettuce.*

8. *Fresh thyme* leaves. (One package from produce section.)

9. *Garlic bulb.*

10. *1 lemon.*

11. *1 large russet potato.*

12. *Bordeaux, Burgundy, or Argentine Carmenere or Super Tuscan wine.*

13. *Mineral water.*

#5 Coq au Vin

1. *Thick sliced bacon.*

2. *1 small whole chicken.*

3. *Olive oil.*

4. *Flour.* (A small bag will do.)

5. *Sugar.* (Small bag.)

6. *Salt and freshly ground black pepper.*

7. *Bay leaf.* (Herb and spice section.)

8. *Dried thyme.* (Herb and spice section.)

9. *Chicken bouillon. (Can or box.)*

10. *Chili sauce or catsup.*

11. *Green salad.*

12. *12 small white onions,* peeled.

13. *Fresh garlic bulb.*

14. *Fresh mushrooms,* whole.

15. *Parsley or fresh thyme sprigs* for garnish.

16. *1 lb. whole carrots.*

17. *Unsalted butter.*

18. *French bread.*

19. *Dry red wine.* (For the dish.)

20. *Brandy.*

21. *Cotes du Rhone or pinot noir.* (For the table.)

22. *Mineral water.*

#6 Grilled Salmon, Couscous and Asparagus

1. 2 pieces *salmon*, approx. 1 lb. total. (I prefer steaks, which are thicker and juicier; however, filets are fine as well.)

2. 1 *lemon.*

3. 1 clove *garlic.*

4. *Scallions* (Green onion).

5. *3/4 lb. asparagus spears.*

6. *Fresh parsley.*

7. *Fresh thyme.*

8. *Extra virgin olive oil.*

9. *Salt and freshly ground pepper.*

10. *Curry powder.* (Spice section)

11. *Couscous.* (Comes in a small box. Found in the rice section.)

12. *White wine vinegar.*

13. *Dijon mustard.*

14. *French Chardonnay from Burgundy, or other dry, unoaked white wine or dry rosé* (at least 12.5% alcohol).

15. *Mineral water.*

#6 Diner al la Walgreens

1. *Spanish olives.*

2. *Extra virgin olive oil.*

3. *Unsalted butter.*

4. *1/2 dozen eggs.*

5. *Swiss cheese.*

6. *Organic Italian penne pasta.*

7. *Bread sticks.*

8. *Can of roma tomatoes.*

9. *Dried oregano. Garlic powder. Onion powder. Red pepper flakes.*

10. *Salt and freshly ground pepper.*

11. *Chocolate ice cream.*

12. *White Bordeaux wine.*

13. *Cognac or brandy.*

14. *Mineral water.*

www.ingramcontent.com/pod-product-compliance
Lightning Source LLC
Chambersburg PA
CBHW041633040426
42447CB00019B/3480